In Front Of or Behind

T0045148

Where's Eddie?

Daniel Nunn

Illustrations by Steve Walker

Hide and Seek

Raintree

Chicago, Illinois

www.capstonepub.com
Visit our website to find out more information about Heinemann-Raintree books.

To order:
Phone 800-747-4992
Visit www.capstonepub.com to browse our catalog and order online.

© 2013 Raintree is an imprint of Capstone Global Library, LLC
Chicago, Illinois

All rights reserved. No part of this publication may be reproduced or transmitted in any form or by any means, electronic or mechanical, including photocopying, recording, taping, or any information storage and retrieval system, without permission in writing from the publisher.

Edited by Dan Nunn, Rebecca Rissman, and Sian Smith
Designed by Joanna Hinton-Malivoire
Picture research by Mica Brancic
Originated by Capstone Global Library, Ltd.
Production by Victoria Fitzgerald

Library of Congress Cataloging-in-Publication Data
Nunn, Daniel.
In front of or behind : where's Eddie? / Daniel Nunn.
p. cm.—(Hide and seek)
Includes bibliographical references and index.
ISBN 978-1-4109-4714-7 (hbk.)
ISBN 978-1-4109-4720-8 (pbk.)
1. Vocabulary—Juvenile literature. I. Title.
PE1449.N774 2012
428.1—dc23 2012000357

Acknowledgments
We would like to thank the following for permission to reproduce photographs: Shutterstock pp.5 (© Losevsky Pavel), 6 (© Dmitry Rukhlenko), 7 (© jomphong), 8 (© nito), 9 (© Tungphoto), 10 (© Ihnatovich Maryia), 11, 12 (© vseb), 13, 14 (© WDG Photo), 15, 16 (© craftvision), 17, 18 (© Tomaz Kunst), 19, 20 (© Valentina R.), 21 (© Tihis), 22 (© Valentina R.), 23 (© Dudarev Mikhail).

Front cover photograph of cupcakes reproduced with permission of Shutterstock (© Elena Talberg).

Every effort has been made to contact copyright holders of any material reproduced in this book. Any omissions will be rectified in subsequent printings if notice is given to the publisher.

2

Printed in the United States 5957

Contents

Meet Eddie the Elephant 4
In Front Of 6
Behind 8
Find Eddie! 10
True or False? 21
Answers and More! 24

Be careful when you hide!
Eddie can hide in places where people can't. Hiding inside things can be very dangerous. Always ask an adult if it is safe first.

Meet Eddie the Elephant

This is Eddie the Elephant.

Eddie loves to play hide and seek!

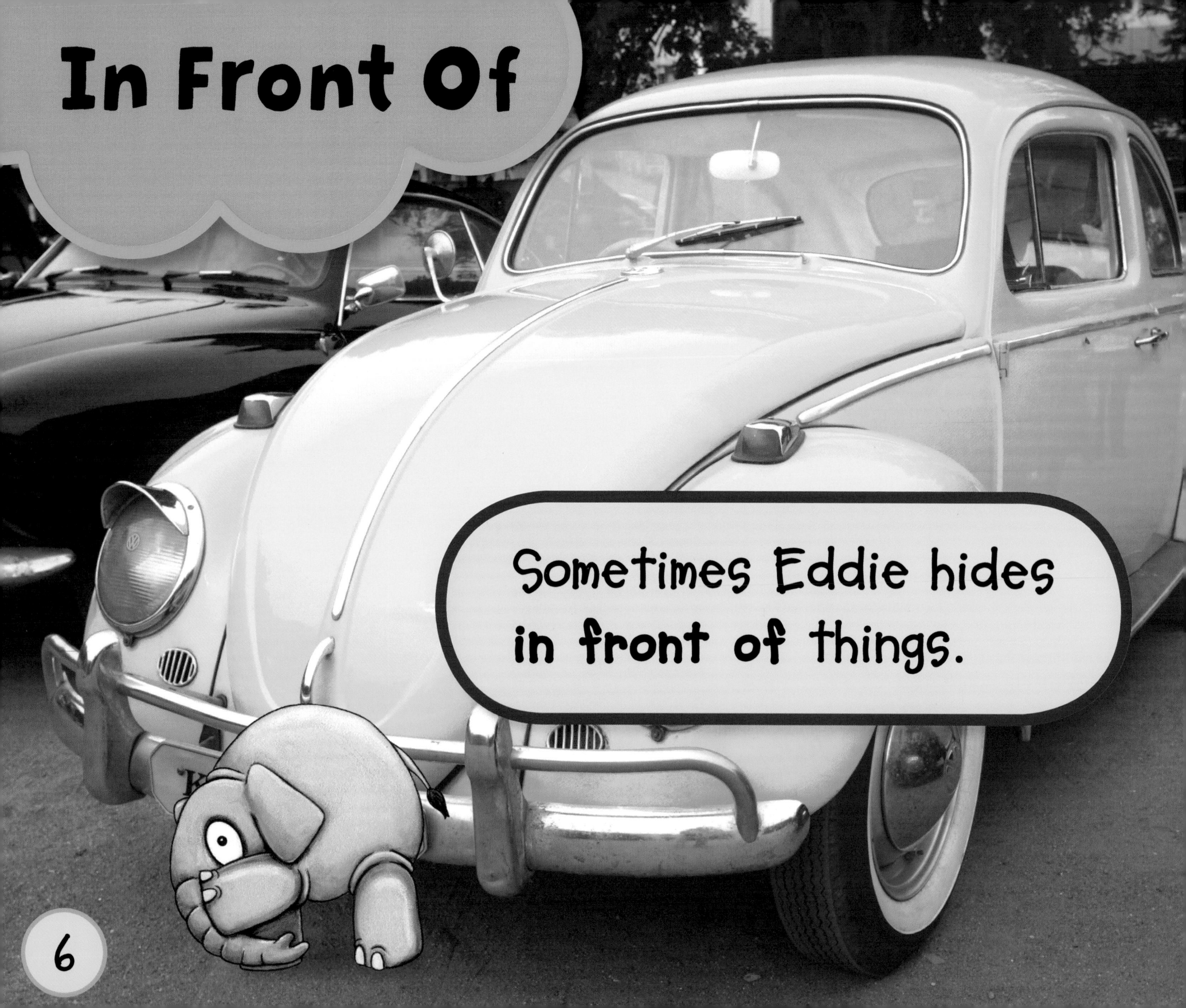
In Front Of
Sometimes Eddie hides in front of things.

When you are **in front of** something, that thing is **behind** you.

Behind

Sometimes Eddie hides **behind** things.

When you are **behind** something,
that thing is **in front of** you.

Find Eddie!

Can you find Eddie?
Count to 10, then off you go!

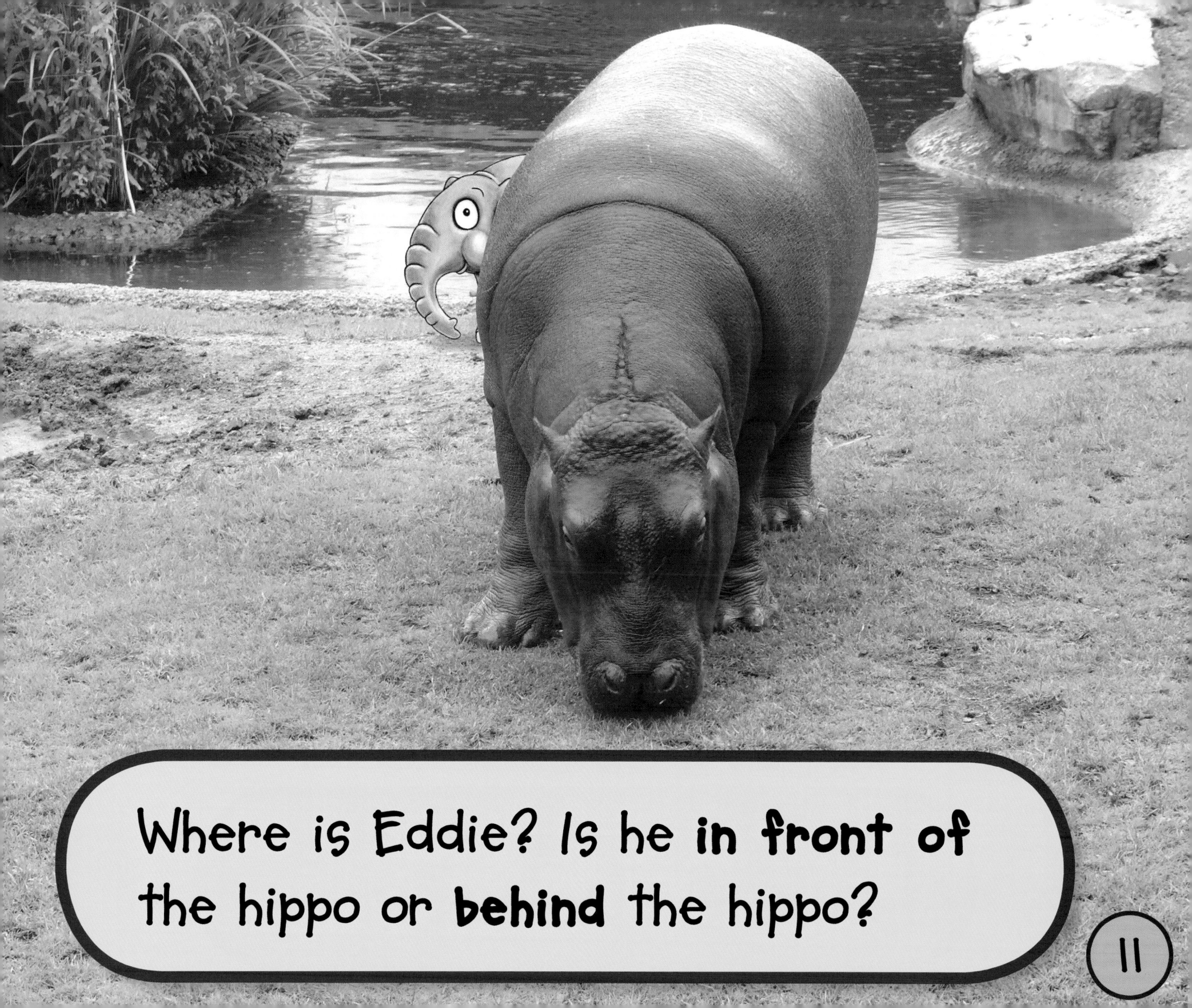

Where is Eddie? Is he **in front of** the hippo or **behind** the hippo?

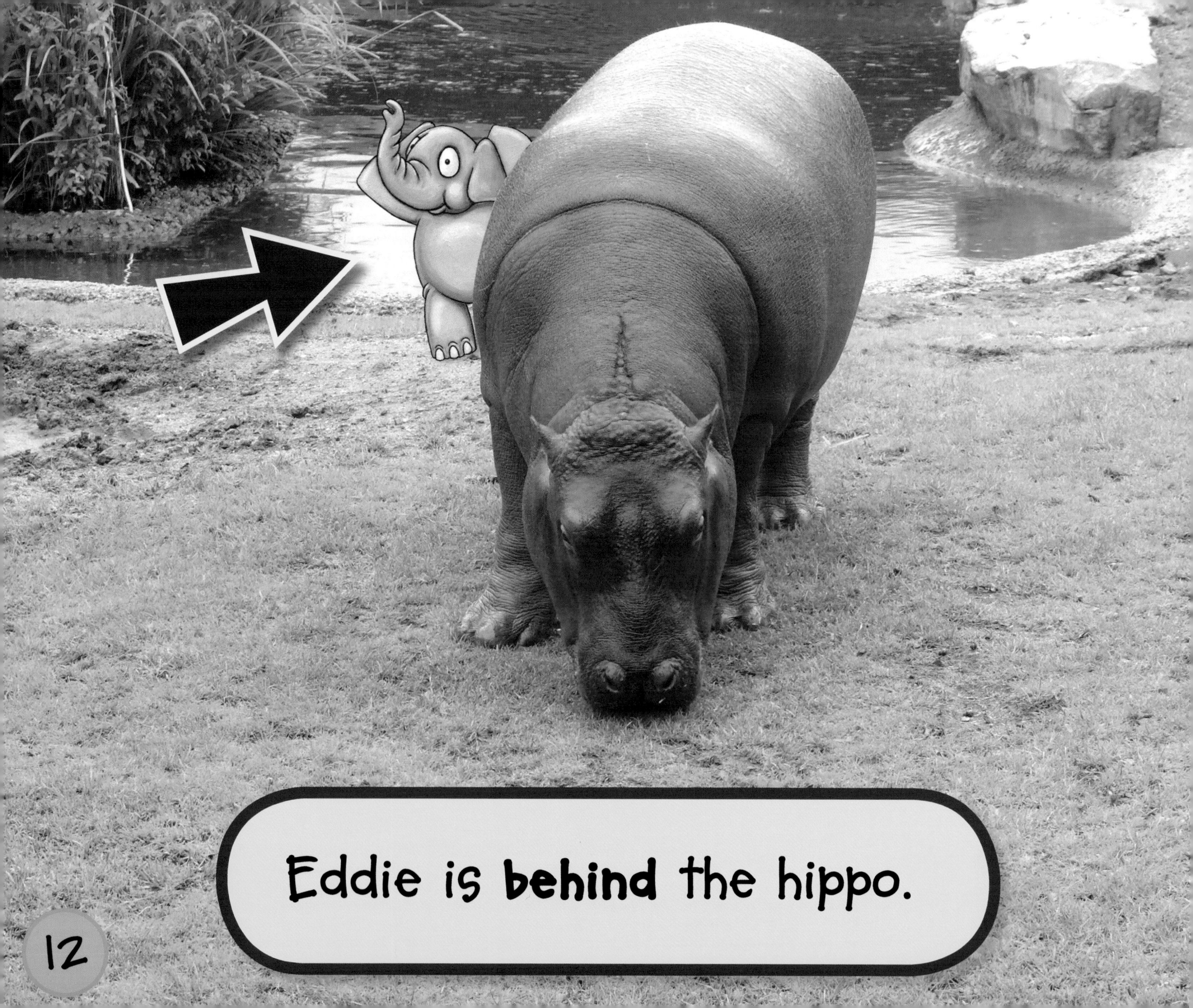

Eddie is **behind** the hippo.

Where is Eddie? Is he **in front of** the tree or **behind** the tree?

Eddie is in front of the tree.

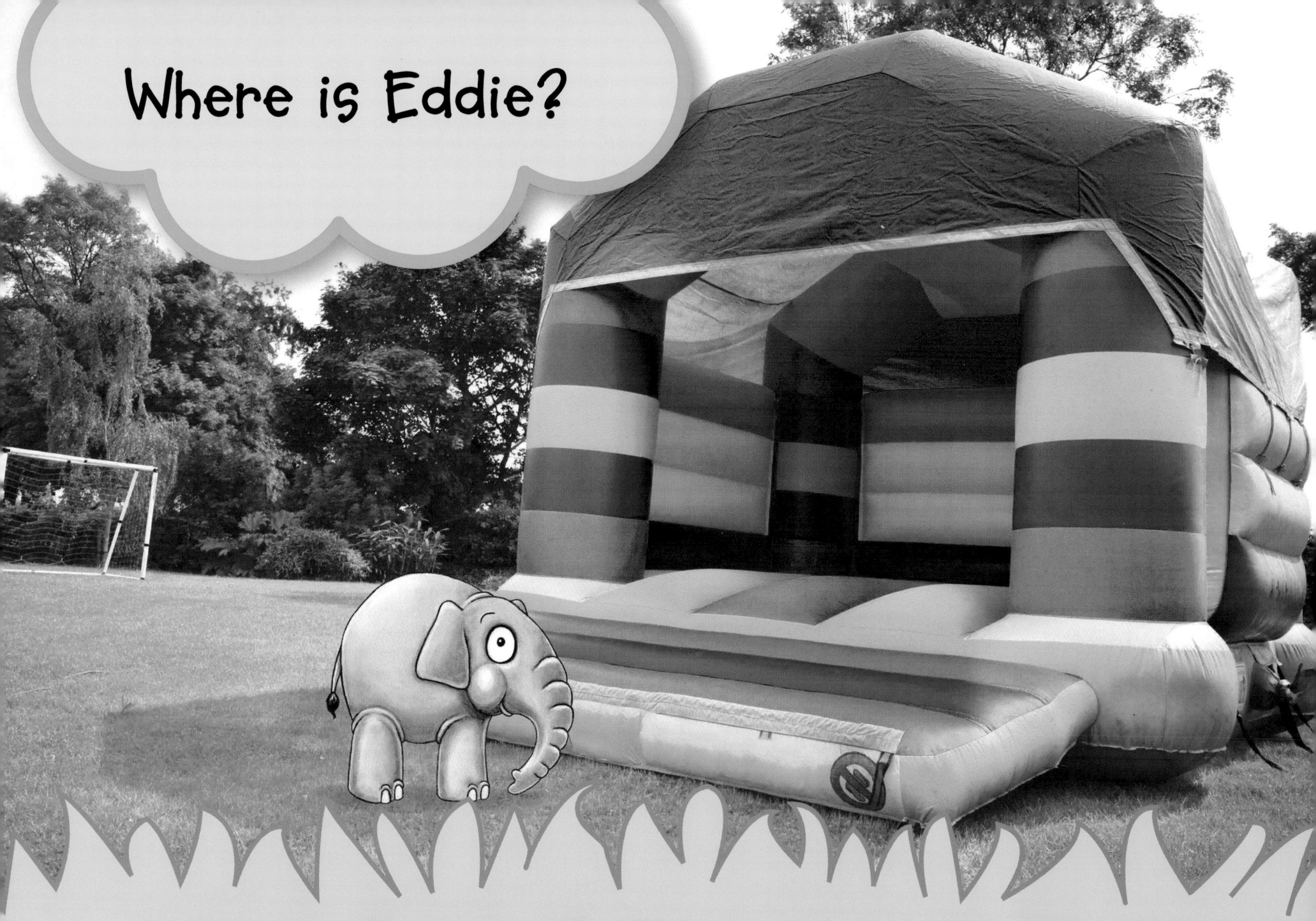

Is he **in front of** the bouncy castle
or **behind** the bouncy castle?

Eddie is **in front of** the bouncy castle.

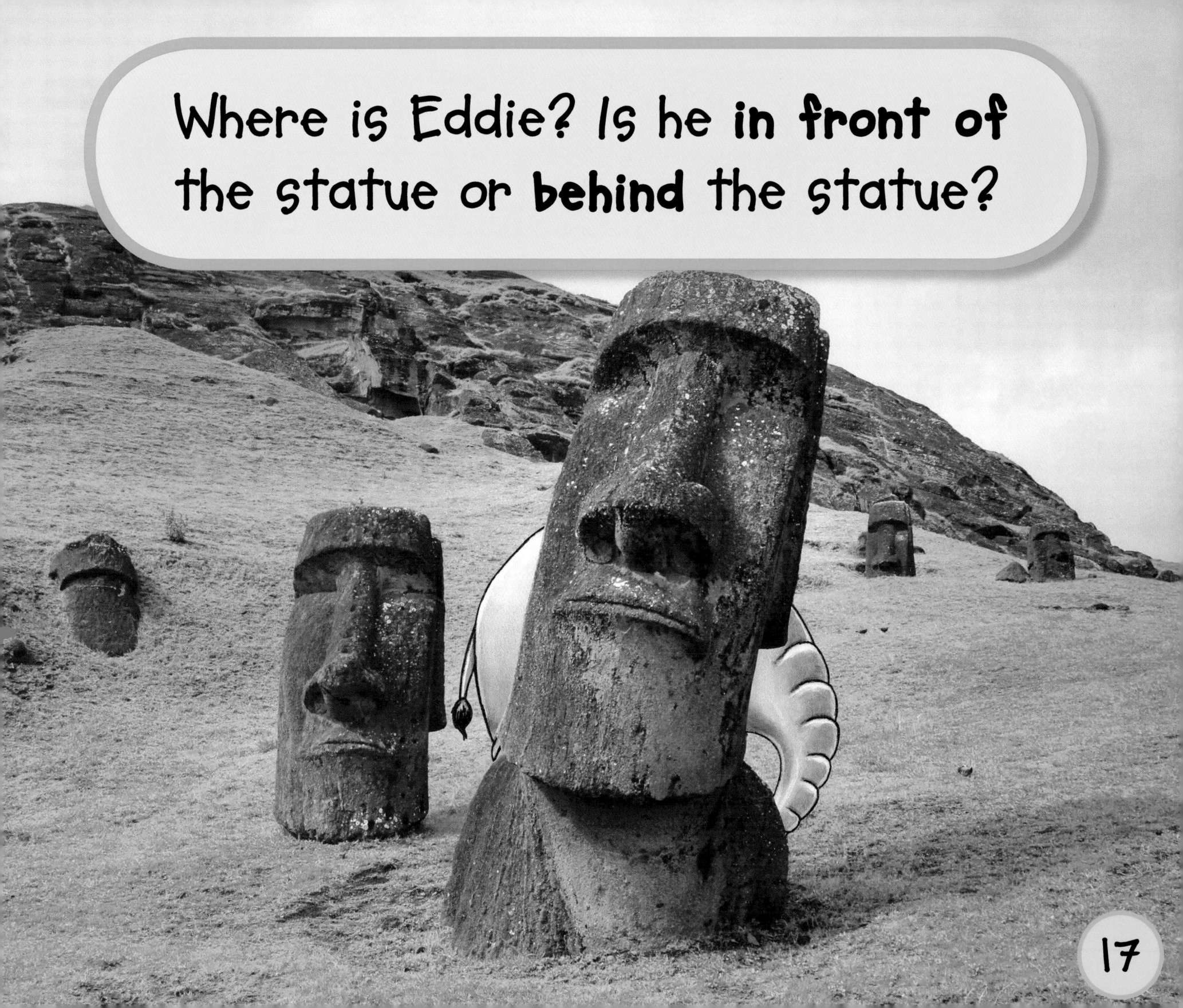

Where is Eddie? Is he **in front of** the statue or **behind** the statue?

Eddie is **behind** the statue.

Where is Eddie? Is he **in front of** the apple or **behind** the apple?

Eddie is **behind** the apple.

True or False?

1. Eddie is **in front of** the snowman. True or false?

You can find the answers on page 24.

2. Eddie is **in front of** the teddy bear. True or false?

3. Eddie is **behind** the bicycle. True or false?

Answers and More!

True or false?

1. True! Eddie is **in front of** the snowman.
2. False! Eddie is **behind** the teddy bear.
3. False! Eddie is **in front of** the bicycle.

Where can Eddie hide next?

Look around the room you are in.

What could Eddie hide **in front of**?

What could Eddie hide **behind**?